Ten Timeless Rules for Life

THINGS EVERY YOUNG PERSON SHOULD KNOW
FOR A PERFECT LAUNCH

Daniel A. Shyti

4 POWER
ENTERPRISES

4 Power Enterprises, LLC
Potomac Falls, Virginia

4 Power Enterprises, LLC
www.4PowerLeadership.com
www.TenTimelessRules.com
Inquiry@4PowerLeadership.com

Cover art & design by Nicole M. Shyti
www.NicoleShyti.com

Book Layout ©2013 BookDesignTemplates.com

Ordering Information for Quantity Sales:

Special discounts are available on quantity purchases by corporations, associations, and others. For details, use the subject line "Special Sales Department" and send an email with your request to the address above.

Ten Timeless Rules for Life/ Daniel A. Shyti. —1st ed (v1).
ISBN 978-0-9897084-4-9

Contents

Dedicated to my son, Daniel A. (Danny) Shyti, Jr.

Who has backbone and conviction.
Who has the courage to pursue his dreams.
Who challenges and frustrates me.
Who makes me a better man for it.
Who I'm proud of immensely.
Who inspires me.
Who I love.

"You are designed for accomplishment, engineered for success, and endowed with the seeds of greatness."

— Zig Ziglar

Introduction

This book is a life guide. It is a way to take a quantum leap forward by leveraging mentorship and applying self-leadership principles on a daily basis. For the book to be useful, you must be open to mentorship. I remember becoming open to mentoring when I:

- Accepted that an "old guy" had something to teach me
- Stopped being hell-bent on making my own mistakes
- Learned that smacking my head into brick walls was no fun
- Started looking at life in a different way.

If you're not open to mentorship, give the book away to someone who is. No harm, no foul. I wish you well. On the other hand, if you're interested, you may...

Start by considering some key questions.

Does your life happen to you or do you make things happen? Do you view yourself as responsible for outcomes based on the choices you make, or do you tend to think that your situation is always someone else's fault? The answers to these questions indicate whether you have a proactive or passive perspective on life. They also point to whether you view yourself as a leader or a follower.

Why is it important to view yourself as a leader? Because leaders are in fact proactive people. They make things happen. Leaders don't sit back and wait for things to happen, unless there's a very good reason for waiting. They stir things up. They do everything they can to achieve a goal or accomplish a mission. They persevere and push forward despite the headwinds they may encounter.

Changing your self-perception from follower to leader puts you in control of your life. It is transformative, and that is the purpose of this book—to create a life-changing impact, whether by completely altering your outlook on life or by reinforcing the positive perspective and habits you may already have.

Can we all be leaders? Absolutely. Must we always lead? Of course not. We must all be followers at some point. There's nothing wrong with being a follower or subordinate. It depends on the situation. At the same time, we are all always leaders. I know that sounds like a contradiction but it's not. You see, by default, we are all always responsible for leading ourselves. We should never surrender our internal perspective of self-leadership even when as part of a team or organization we fall in behind someone else who has formal leadership responsibility. This keeps you focused on remaining a proactive person.

At some point, you may choose to pursue a formal leadership position either at work, on a sports team, or in your community. Because you have developed the right mindset of leadership, you will be able to rise to the challenge. As a bonus, maintaining a leadership mindset makes you a better follower because you are able to see the world through the lens of leadership. Therefore, you're able to recognize good leadership when you see it. When the leader encounters challenges, you are also able to empathize and offer constructive suggestions.

Here's the first tip I can offer you about leadership—authenticity. Authenticity in leadership is the water that quenches the thirst of willing followers. Authenticity promotes trust in a leader and people need to trust their leader. In numerous research surveys, trustworthiness always percolates to the top as the quality people value most in a leader. But trust can be shattered, especially when authenticity is compromised. Is the leader actually the kind of person that he portrays himself to be? If you've ever discovered that a leader you've been following is a fraud and routinely deceives people, then you've experienced how quickly trust evaporates.

In the spirit of authenticity, I decided to take an inward look at my core beliefs. What emerged is this book: *Ten Timeless Rules for Life—Things Every Young Person Should Know for a Perfect Launch*. The Ten Timeless Rules have served as a guide for my life every day, though frankly, I didn't always know I was following them. These are the rules that served as the foundation for my success and I'm pleased to share them with you in this book. In each chapter, I explain the essence of a rule and provide an explanation of its relevance to leadership.

As you read them, keep in mind that just like you, I'm a work in progress. I'm not perfect and I never pretend for a second that I am. Sometimes I even come up short in living according to my own rules. Leadership is not about being perfect. The focus of leadership is to develop and exercise the will to pursue perfection relentlessly. It's important to understand that living and succeeding by these rules is eminently attainable. By using these rules, you too can enjoy the same success I've achieved and more if you make the decision to apply yourself. It's that simple.

I firmly believe in learning from others by modeling their success and avoiding their mistakes. The Ten Timeless Rules represent what has worked for me throughout thirty-plus years in professional life. These rules have helped me advance and succeed in good times and bad. Will they work for you? You decide. It's your life and the beauty of life is we all have free will to make our own choices. We should also have the fortitude to accept responsibility for the paths we choose. Hopefully, the experience shared through these rules will help you make better choices—both professionally and personally. This is useful knowledge.

I make no apologies for my beliefs, but I'm always open to learning. Life is a journey and it's a good idea to know with whom you're traveling. This leads me to a few questions for you to think about.

What do you believe?

Have you considered what your personal constitution is? What are the rules by which you live? A sound value system is essential for positive leadership. It's one of the first things I discuss in my previous book, *4 Power Leadership: Your Pathway to Leadership Success.* Do you have the courage and commitment to write down what you believe and to defend it?

The young are our future leaders.

The following is my favorite leadership quote. I have yet to discover a thought that more clearly explains what it means to be a leader:

> *"If your actions inspire others to dream more, learn more, do more, and become more, you are a leader."*
>
> — *John Quincy Adams*

If you're a college-age person just starting or about to graduate from college, this book is primarily written for you, but it can also apply to anyone who wants to course correct their life. Even if you have no aspiration for formal leadership in the future, learning to think like a leader can create profound change. Leaders are proactive, self-driven, and fully accountable people who accept responsibility for their own actions. Leaders don't make excuses. They're about establishing and attaining goals. Leaders set the example and act honorably every day.

My source of inspiration.

Inspiration can come from anywhere. Something happens and instantly your brain can be triggered into a creative response. I make it a habit to follow my inspiration. I recommend that you pay attention to your "inspired thoughts" and make a habit of writing them down or capturing them in your smartphone as soon as they pop into your head.

This book was inspired by the "energetic" conversations I (a Baby Boomer father) typically have with my Millennial son. We talk about a lot of things. He's one of just a handful of individuals with whom I speak regularly on deep subjects. His mind functions at a very high intellectual level. I have to run to keep up, and we never have a dull conversation.

His views don't always square with mine. However, through our conversations, we influence each other. His thinking shifts and mine does too.

Why Ten Rules? It just worked out that way. Are they the only things I believe? No, there's more. The Ten Timeless Rules for Life are just the first things that came to mind. It felt right to stop there for now.

Where to from here?

Today, the quality of our social discourse has deteriorated to an alarming low. It seems everyone is more interested in agenda advancement than exchanging ideas, creating understanding, and solving problems. It's up to you, the leaders of tomorrow, to pull us back from this destructive pattern and restore some civility to our conversations. Respectfully sharing what you truly believe is a step in the right direction. Backing your beliefs with facts and a rational perspective is the best foundation for constructive exchange. Don't be afraid to define what you believe and develop the capacity to defend it with logic instead of raw emotion. Your belief system is your foundation as a leader.

We can express our beliefs with tolerance for differing views. Just because someone disagrees with you that doesn't automatically make them a "hater." These days, it seems that we are ridiculously quick to affix that label to people who don't view the world through the same lens as us. A disagreement or criticism about behavior is not automatically an attack on your character.

Stay open and listen. When someone presents a different way and his or her logic is sound, are you willing to adjust your thinking? Are you open to embracing better answers, or will you stick with flawed thinking because you've closed yourself off to different points of view? This takes us back to the question you should answer for yourself: What do you believe and why?

Dan Shyti
Potomac Falls, Virginia
April 2018

CHAPTER 1

Rule 1: God Exists: Here's How I Know

"In view of such harmony in the cosmos which I, with my limited human mind, am able to recognize, there are yet people who say there is no God."

— *Albert Einstein*

Wow! What a place to start—one of the biggest questions that most of us ask ourselves. This is not a religious book, but I do firmly believe in God and I believe that trusting in God fundamentally shapes the course of our lives. So why not address the most important thing first.

There are two points of logic to back my belief. First, everything we see in our observable universe always seems to have some purpose. The more I examine and learn about the physical world, the more I marvel at how everything fits together. Every cell in your body has a purpose. The moon, sun, and stars have a purpose. Volcanoes have a purpose. Squirrels have a purpose. Everything seems to have a purpose except—mosquitoes. I hate them. When my time comes to meet the good Lord, I hope to ask him, "What were you thinking when you created mosquitoes?" Regardless, I'm sure mosquitoes somehow fit into His grand plan somewhere because everything does indeed have a purpose.

The more I learn about nature, the earth, and the universe, the more I'm amazed at how interdependent and balanced everything is. The order and balance of everything leads me to believe that there is intent behind everything we see. Intent strengthens my belief in a creator God.

Here's my second point. Scientists believe that the universe came into existence from a single infinitesimally dense point. As the Big Bang Theory suggests, a vast explosion with a potency we can't even imagine triggered a series of seemingly random cause-and-effect events, ultimately resulting in you, me, and every other living and non-living thing in the universe. The key point here is cause and effect.

In science, absolutely everything hinges on cause and effect. It's an immutable law. If you assume that there is no Creator, believing that the Big Bang occurred with no initial cause is illogical. So, what was the primary cause? To argue that an effect happened without a cause is illogical and contradicts science.

You may say then, "Where does God come from? What caused Him?" No one knows that answer. But I certainly find belief in God far more logical than a scientist telling me that the first effect happened without a cause!

Can the existence of God be absolutely proven according to rigorous scientific methods? No. Belief in God does come down to a matter of faith. But to me, a preponderance of the evidence points in the direction of a Creator. The circumstantial evidence of creation is proof of his existence.

The Big Bang Theory, which seems very plausible, does not disprove the existence of God. It simply represents a peek into His awesome methods. God in His infinite wisdom calculated all the expected results of His ideas and then set creation in motion. I see no contradiction between science and believing in God. In fact, it was a Catholic Priest, Georges Lemaître, who is credited as the father of the Big Bang Theory.

Even Albert Einstein believed in God, though not in the traditional sense of a personal God. Consider the following thought from Einstein:

> *"The human mind, no matter how highly trained, cannot grasp the universe. We are in the position of a little child, entering a huge library whose walls are covered to the ceiling with books in many different tongues. The child knows that someone must have written those books. It does not know who or how. It does not understand the languages in which they are written. The child notes a definite plan in the arrangement of the books, a mysterious order, which it does not comprehend, but only dimly suspects. That, it seems to me, is the attitude of the human mind, even the greatest and most cultured, toward God. We see a universe marvelously arranged, obeying certain laws, but we understand the laws only dimly. Our limited minds cannot grasp the mysterious force that sways the constellations."* [1]

To believe that everything we see is the result of mere randomness is like taking all the parts of a clock, throwing them into a paper bag, shaking the bag vigorously, and then expecting a fully assembled clock to somehow emerge. The odds of that occurring are zero — the same odds as the universe being the result of mere randomness. You and I and the universe were meant to exist. Give God His due.

Why is Rule 1 relevant to leadership?

We are spiritual creatures. Deep down inside, we have a yearning to reconnect with our Creator. When you deny this need, you

---

[1] Viereck, George Sylvester. "Glimpses of the Great". Duckworth, 1930. p. 372-373

create a void inside yourself. In nature, voids are always filled with something. When you deny God, what will fill the void within you? Surely, you will replace God with a god of a different sort. Something else will become the center of your universe.

In the seminars I teach, I always encourage leaders to take the journey within and resolve lingering issues. The purpose is for the leader to become a complete and healed person to the greatest degree possible. A whole leader is a well-grounded leader.

I view belief in God as a prerequisite to becoming a complete and balanced person. To me, a leader that has his values and life firmly grounded in God is a leader who acknowledges that there are bigger things in life than himself. A well-grounded leader is much more likely to be a positive force in society, on any team, or in any organization.

But most important of all, when you believe in a loving creator God, you are never alone. Even in your darkest hour when all you may feel is loneliness and despair, there is someone who loves you. I've been in the dumps many times, and this thought has always pulled me back from the edge and sustained me.

CHAPTER 2

Rule 2: Focus on the Big Stuff

"'Love the Lord your God with all your heart and with all your soul and with all your mind.' This is the first and greatest commandment. And the second is like it: 'Love your neighbor as yourself.' All the Law and the Prophets hang on these two commandments."

— Jesus Christ

Hey, I thought you said this wasn't a religious book? If you thought that, I can understand why, but again, it's not. Rule 2 is not about pushing religion, it's about finding your spiritual truth and center. Read on and I'll also show you why the quotation forms the perfect self-leadership and ethics framework for each facet of your life.

The quotation above is the essence of what you really must know about religion. If we did exactly what it is says and nothing more, we would probably be better off than many people who go to church every Sunday. It's about how we should handle our relationship with God and dealing fairly with all the people we encounter in business and our personal lives. That's the Big Stuff and the core of what actually matters after you strip away all the window dressing of most religions.

The quotation above might be controversial to some, but before you move on, read it again. Take time to fully absorb the quotation. Let the profound thoughts it expresses lead your heart and all your priorities will fall into place. Structure your life around these two commandments and you will achieve more harmony in your life than you could have ever imagined.

Maybe you have trouble accepting these thoughts because it was Jesus who said them. Okay. Disregard the source for now and ask yourself why you might otherwise object to the quotation. Do you know that variations of this quotation exist in every major world religion? Truth is truth regardless of who says it.

I'm well aware that organized religions demand more of their followers than these two simple commandments. The problem is that we can often become so caught up in dogma to the detriment of what matters most. The Big Stuff is then often obscured or ignored. In comparison to the profoundness of Jesus' words, isn't everything else just needless complexity? How many people do you know that attend their house of worship with a regularity that rivals Old Faithful? How often do you see those same people not living by the two greatest commandments?

Many faithful people find value in congregating and professing their love for God. We are social creatures that need to belong to groups. It's in our nature. There are also many religious groups that focus on faith and good works. If you are part of one of these groups, then you're probably in a good place.

The media often sensationalizes the scoundrels that perpetuate scandal, sexual abuse, and violence connected to religious groups. It's ironic that when people fail, somehow God also gets attacked. This contributes to an increase in agnosticism and atheism, which are more prevalent than ever among young people.

Heinous acts committed in the name of religion have the effect of turning young people away from God and that's truly sad. This is especially true when religion-driven rivalry leads to violence. People are quick to spout that "more people have been killed in the name of religion than in any other cause." Whether true or not, they use this glib and worn out premise to justify that God is nothing but a fairytale.

The stream of negative press about religion is further combined with blind acceptance that science replaces God. It's no wonder that young people have great difficulty countering this ever-persistent one-two punch to faith. So what's my advice?

If you made it past Rule 1, you should not have a problem with Rule 2. Don't sacrifice a belief in God because you are somehow turned off by organized religion and convinced it is bad. If you have trouble accepting organized religion, then keep it simple, focus on the Big Stuff, and let God lead your heart. If you are a member of an organized religious group, then be a force in keeping everyone focused on the Big Stuff.

Why is Rule 2 relevant to leadership?

The Big Stuff is guidance for your entire life. First, it reinforces belief in God. As I said in Rule 1, belief in God makes you a complete and balanced person. God fills the spiritual void in all of us. In the context of leadership, Rule 2 also lays the foundation for ethical leadership and all our dealings with others. One of the foremost requirements of a leader is to be fair and just to the people you lead. "Love your neighbor as yourself" establishes that foundation. Treat others as you would like to be treated in your personal life and the workplace.

For example, would you want your boss to favor others regardless of your contribution to the team? If not, then don't play favorites with the people you lead. When you focus on the Big Stuff, you have a built-in GPS for your life. All your actions as a leader will be based on the most important rules of all. That's powerful. That's the root of positive leadership.

CHAPTER 3

Rule 3: Don't Waste Time Pursuing the Unknowable

"I know why I am here and my only real focused goal is to live each day to the fullest and to try and honor God and be an encouragement to others. What the future holds is firmly in God's hands, and I am very happy about that!"

— *Ken Hensley*

Why the heck am I here? That's a question we've probably all pondered at some point in our lives. We can make assumptions, but unlike all the things that we observe and for which we can discern a clear purpose, we humans struggle mightily with finding our own individual purpose. This struggle has triggered movements, books, and a plethora of seminars on finding your "why." Good luck with that. You're chasing your tail. Here are the facts about your life's purpose.

We may find an occupation on this earth that we truly enjoy. We may excel so greatly at it that we reach astonishing heights of success. Yet, can you truly say that this thing that gives you so much success is your cosmic purpose? I think that's presumptuous and even a bit arrogant. If you're energized by your occupation and it gives you great joy, more power to you. You have found fulfillment, and you're in a select minority. Still, don't assume that it's your purpose for living, because you don't truly know.

Billy Joel is my favorite musical artist of all time. I grew up listening to his music. He's had dozens of hit records, made millions of dollars through his art, and continues to sell out arenas to this day. Yet, can even he truly say that all those accomplishments constitute his cosmic purpose? What if all those things are secondary?

In 1985 Billy released a song titled, "You're Only Human (Second Wind)." The song deals with youth suicide — something that continues to plague us today. I wonder if that song has saved anyone's life through its inspirational words. If it saved just one life, don't you think it outweighs all of Billy's other accomplishments? Could writing that song possibly be his cosmic purpose? We don't know, but God has His ways.

Young people today are more focused than ever on the need for purpose and meaning. Unfortunately, this preoccupation can sometimes lead to "life paralysis." When confronted with a task as daunting as finding your life's purpose, you can quickly become overwhelmed with the thought, "Man, I better get this right!" As a result, decision and direction can be put off indefinitely in a vicious cycle of second-guessing.

If you're absolutely hung up on finding your "why," may I suggest that you reread Rule 2 until the answer becomes obvious? Spending too much time on searching for your "why" beyond Rule 2 will only reduce you to an existential dog chasing his existential tail.

Throw yourself into something you like.

When undecided about what you should do for an occupation or what your next career move should be, pick a direction based on what interests you most. What do you like? Move out smartly, and do something positive related to what you like. Sustain that action with persistent effort. Action is better than inaction. Standing still is a self-defining fate. Doing nothing and remaining indecisive seals your fate. Action creates feedback and opportunity. At worst, by taking action, you'll identify what you don't like.

There's a difference between meaning, fulfillment, and purpose. You can find meaning and fulfillment in just about any career, though you can't assume it's your cosmic purpose. If you approach life with the heart of an artist, fulfillment follows. An artist pours himself into his work. In essence, his work and his being are inseparable. You can create this type of devotion to any profession. No matter what your current job is, do it from the heart — fulfillment and as much wealth as you want will follow.

Why is Rule 3 relevant to leadership?

Endless ruminating and searching for your "personal why" can lead to paralysis in decision-making. Paralysis and leadership do not mix. They cannot coexist inside the leader's mind. Leaders must maintain a clear focus on the path ahead in order to lead others and themselves. Leadership is about taking action, not pointless pondering. Rule 2 provides all the "personal why" that anyone needs. So, move out and get going!

CHAPTER 4

Rule 4: Value Knowledge of History

"Most of us spend too much time on the last twenty-four hours and too little on the last six thousand years."

— *Will Durant*

All people since the dawn of humanity have 99.5% of their DNA in common. That means that we are very close to identical in physiological make up. That 0.5% difference accounts for all variations such as gender, height, hair and skin color, strength, speed, intellect, etc. The Population Reference Bureau guesstimates that 108 billion people have been born since mankind's appearance on earth some 50,000 years ago. Guess what? We are all 99.5% identical.

The internal combustion engine of emotion powers human behavior. Occasionally we benefit from turbo boosts of logic and genius, but predominantly we are emotional creatures. The basic behavioral drivers that cause people to act a certain way under certain conditions haven't changed one bit. Our emotional responses are heavily influenced by hardwired physiological factors. The fight-or-flight instinct is a good example of this.

With all that genetic commonality and all the personal interaction of all those people from decades, centuries, and millennia past, what is the likelihood that the present-day human experience is completely unique? About zero! This is the unique benefit of understanding history. It gives you knowledge of what drives people at a personal level. When you understand what drives people you become a better leader even if you're an army of one.

Certainly, from a technological standpoint, the world looks very different than it did just 200 years ago, and the pace of change is accelerating at an astonishing rate. We also have a much larger population than ever before. However, basic human behavior is as constant as the North Star.

Why study history?

I once heard a comment regarding history: "Why do I have to know something that I can Google?" Life doesn't always allow you to stop and search for facts. The pace of life requires a certain level of knowledge at the ready to quickly make decisions and respond to challenges. Also, Googling facts is not the same as understanding connections between events, cultures, and people. Proactive study of history can be mind-blowing when you learn how much we have in common with our ancestors.

It stands to reason that history is the repository for the future as well as the past. To understand the past is like being able to see around a corner. In the field of human relations, nothing is ever truly new. Niccolò Machiavelli, the Renaissance writer, historian, and politician observed the consistency of human nature. He wrote the following in his *Discourses*:

Whoever considers the past and the present will readily observe that all cities and all peoples... ever have been animated by the same desires and the same passions; so that it is easy, by diligent study of the past, to foresee what is likely to happen in the future in any republic, and to apply those remedies that were used by the ancients, or not finding any that were employed by them, to devise new ones from the similarity of events.

We have a Republic—if we can keep it.

The Founding Fathers of the United States were remarkable men who, after winning a revolution, could easily have established a king or dictator to rule over their spoils. Instead, they did something remarkable and unprecedented. They gave power away to the people.

These brilliant and learned men were devoted students of history. They looked to the past as they shaped the American constitution. As they formed our laws, they leaned on their knowledge of how tyranny is spawned. They developed a system, a republic, to ensure that tyranny would not swallow our country. So far, the constitution they created has survived for 230 years and counting, though it is constantly under assault. (But that's another subject entirely.)

Their genius, forethought, and insight were based on examination of the past. They learned that concentration of power leads to corruption and ultimately to tyranny. They knew that oppression suffocates our common human aspirations for a better life. That's why they gave us divided government through the separation of powers.

Proceed with caution. If you extinguish the light of history, you'll be navigating your future in the dark.

Why is Rule 4 relevant to leadership?

Acquiring a strong working knowledge of history can serve two purposes for you. First, you'll gain insight into what works and what doesn't. If you know history, you'll be armed with test cases from the volumes of human experience. This makes it much harder for people to fool you into thinking that a flawed course of action is valid when history testifies to its failure.

Second, history is an invaluable source of mentorship for an emerging leader. If you want to become an exceptional leader, read as much as you can about great leaders. Read about leaders in all types of contexts. The sound principles of leadership are transferable across situations, environments, and periods. The greats of old are as relevant today as they were in their time. The connecting factor is the constant of human nature.

CHAPTER 5

Rule 5: Neither Loathe Money Nor Love It

"Money is only a tool. It will take you wherever you wish, but it will not replace you as the driver."

— *Ayn Rand*

D evelop a healthy respect for money as a tool and nothing more. Money gives you choices. The more money you have, the more freedom of choice you gain. Yet, large swaths of our young population have somehow developed a loathing for money. Why?

Many young people may have observed their parents attempting the slippery scramble up the corporate ladder. They watched as their parents worked long hours to provide a better life for their kids and pay off all their accumulated status symbols. Where did the scramble lead? The parents probably collided with a midlife crisis where they sat and wondered, "What was the point of it all?" Along the way, their children decided the corporate climb wasn't worth it, but along with that assessment, a loathing of money somehow also took root.

Another possibility is that many young people may view attainment of wealth as something remote and out of reach for them. It therefore becomes easier to detest something they think they can never have. They develop a loathing for people with money who live in comfort and relative freedom. It's a form of jealousy shrouded in false higher virtue.

Still, others may place a much higher premium on living as they please outside the demands of a more structured career. I can understand wanting to first design the life you want and then figuring out how you can make money at it. That's a fine order of priorities. In the end, living the life you want is what matters most for happiness. However, proper emphasis should also be placed on the need to earn enough money to not only sustain yourself but to actually build wealth.

By building wealth, I mean creating a robust savings plan that removes the stress of living paycheck-to-paycheck. A substantial financial cushion helps you absorb the blows life throws at you in an unexpected crisis. Having a nest-egg also creates choices and opens your life to a broad array of opportunities.

Regardless of the cause, lack of proper emphasis on earning potential has contributed to a situation where millions of college students graduate every year with unmarketable degrees and Everest-sized debt. As the strains of Pomp and Circumstance fade, new graduates eagerly unfurl their diplomas only to realize they're actually holding promissory notes. Now they're burdened with paying back huge sums while working in jobs that sometimes pay the pittance of minimum wage. Often, these jobs could easily still have been obtained if they hadn't gone to college at all.

There's nothing wrong with pursuing your interests. But before you plunk down $100,000 for that major in "high-altitude basket weaving studies," you may want to consider the return on investment and probability of finding employment. This doesn't mean you have to abandon something that interests you. Just don't be duped into paying a ridiculous tuition for something that won't help you pay your bills. Find yourself an expert "high-altitude basket weaver" and persuade him or her to mentor you. It's cheaper and probably more fun.

The flipside of money loathing is money loving. People who sacrifice anything for a bigger paycheck are equally—if not even more—misguided. They spend their life in pursuit of the next big payday, missing birthdays, anniversaries, and the kids' band performances. When the fog of the chase lifts, what's left? What memories do they have? "I wish I had made one more sales call" won't be the thought that crosses their mind on their deathbed.

Why is Rule 5 relevant to leadership?

Leaders should not be hung up on money. If money is the primary focus for a person seeking a leadership position, then that person is leading for the wrong reasons. Positive leaders maintain a balanced view of money. They do expect just rewards for their work, but they don't use money as their prime motivator.

Leaders who have not properly addressed their own earning potential and compensation can easily become distracted and subject to temptations that would not arise if their own financial situation were well under control.

Clearly, balance is the key. Money is essential. You need it to create the desired degree of comfort in your life, but if you're ever in a situation where you must choose between loving money or loving God, the choice is clear—love God. Back to Rule 2.

CHAPTER 6

Rule 6: Trade Your Time for as Much Money as You Can Get

"A man without ambition is dead. A man with ambition but no love is dead. A man with ambition and love for his blessings here on earth is ever so alive."

— Pearl Bailey

You may think that Rule 6 is a total contradiction of Rule 5, but it's not. Rule 6 is actually about self-worth, value creation, efficiency, and balanced ambition—not greed. Trading your time for as much money as you can get is fundamental for surviving and thriving in today's world. It's especially important if one day you intend to start and support a family.

I'm not saying that everyone should strive to become some Wall Street high roller. Maximizing your earnings per unit of time applies to whatever line of work you're in. If you're an artist and you can sell a painting for $100, don't settle for $20. Your time and talent are valuable, and they're all you have to trade. Besides, the best way to ensure that you can continue doing something you love is to make it pay you well.

There's an important exception to Rule 6. There are people who are called to a life of service to whom this rule does not directly apply. A shining example is Mother Theresa. She worked tirelessly for nearly her entire life on behalf of the poor and downtrodden without seeking any money for herself. If you are called to such a life, God bless you.

The context of Rule 6 is for those who are seeking a mainstream life in the common economy. For those in a life of service to others, you can modify the application of this rule by trading your time for the greatest benefit you can provide to others. Interestingly, if you are successful at boosting your earnings through application of Rule 6, you can still serve others because you'll have resources that you can donate whenever you want.

Poverty is hideous.

When I was a child, my dad would occasionally share stories of his childhood. He was born into abject poverty in Albania at the end of World War I. Starvation among the peasants was common. There were days when all he had to eat was a single onion. While he had no shoes for his feet, he also had to endure mockery from the children of the lords who controlled the country. His stories impressed upon me that poverty is hideous. Through strength of will and ingenuity, he was able to lift himself out of what seemed like a hopeless situation.

You have the power.

In modern-day America, we are still blessed with opportunity in spite of all the problems we have. So why not maximize your earning potential? Everyone has the power to improve his or her economic condition. You just have to decide that you want to.

Never waste an opportunity to learn a new marketable skill. The more skills you have, the easier it will be to trade your time for increasing amounts of money. This is the heart of value creation. The more skilled you are, the more valuable you become. As your personal economic value rises, the easier it will be to increase your income per unit of time.

Skills can be acquired in multiple ways. It doesn't have to be through expensive formal secondary education. You can become more valuable through on-the-job training, certifications paid for by your employer, grants, self-teaching, and of course—mentorship.

There are times when you may intentionally go through a period of low earnings while you "retool" for higher pay down the road. This is an investment that will yield a future return and is actually consistent with the concept of Rule 6. The reward is just delayed.

Be wise to how the system works.

Free markets will always seek efficiency in that an acquirer always tries to gain an asset for the least possible cost. If you don't take a counterbalancing approach, the market will eat you alive. Once you discover that you are unfairly compensated, bitterness takes hold. You'll then hit a dead end terminating in anxiety, frustration, and instability. Ensuring that you are fairly compensated for the value you deliver creates stability in your life and the lives of your loved ones.

Don't be afraid to start visualizing the success you want and keep reaching higher throughout your productive life. You can decide how much of your time you want to trade away and for how much, but ignore this rule at your own peril. If you want to reap you must sow.

Why is Rule 6 relevant to leadership?

Rule 6 keeps you proactive in your career planning. It forces you to stay current in your skills and ensures you have the competitive edge that you need to thrive. This is part of your personal leadership. Remember, you are responsible for leading yourself.

Rule 6 also keeps you sensitive to the needs of others. If you do end up in a formal leadership position where you manage the financial compensation of others, this rule helps develop a keen understanding of the relationship between value, reward, and return on investment. Also, it will help you coach others in developing their skills so they can provide greater value to your business. Remember that just like you're trying to trade your time for as much money as you can get, so are others. Making sure the exchange is equitable is a key to sound leadership as you'll see in Rule 7.

CHAPTER 7

Rule 7: Master the Equitable Exchange

"Fairness is not an attitude. It's a professional skill that must be developed and exercised."

— Brit Hume

In business, as in life, altruism is as common as unicorns, Sasquatch, and honest politicians. When I deliver that line in my seminars, it always gets a laugh and everyone's attention. Altruism means "the unselfish concern for the welfare of others; selflessness." True altruism is extremely rare in business and in all aspects of life. Most people focus on themselves. Enlightened leaders focus on the equitable exchange.

If you look back at Rule 2, Jesus didn't say, "Love your neighbor more than yourself." He didn't say, "Take care of your neighbor to your own detriment." He said, "Love your neighbor as yourself." He placed you on equal footing with your neighbor. He implied that you have needs and so does your neighbor. In all our relationships, we should therefore work toward meeting each other's needs through equitable exchange.

When you want something, you should always be thinking about what you can give in return that's fair. It's also not a sin or somehow less noble to believe that when people give something, they usually expect something in return. Sometimes all that's required is politeness, heartfelt gratitude, and a simple thank you.

Sometimes people perform what we view as a completely selfless act. I agree that at times there are people who are extraordinarily generous with their time and treasure, but I believe they are still receiving a payback. That can come from a simple sense of satisfaction in knowing they helped someone. They could possibly be fulfilling a form of spiritual obligation. Their return may be small in monetary terms. In that sense, we may call their act selfless, but isn't their emotional satisfaction the return they were looking for?

In October 2015, Jack Dorsey, CEO of Twitter "gave back" about one-third of his Twitter shares (7 million shares worth about $200M) so the company could fund employee bonus pools. Several talking heads on CNBC quickly called the move "altruistic." Was it?

The reality is that Dorsey is a smart businessman. He must have thought, "I'd rather have a smaller share of something big than a bigger share of something small." His action was not altruistic in the least. It was purely transactional and calculated based on potential financial gain to him and his shareholders. The fact is Dorsey made an equitable exchange — an investment. He is banking on his shares serving as motivation for his employees to innovate and grow the company. In exchange, the employees get to own part of the company and increase their wealth. It's a win-win and a gutsy leadership move, but certainly not altruistic.

Living by an expectation of altruism is bogus. It helps breed a culture of entitlement. It's dishonest and selfish to expect someone to give to you without an obligation to give something back. An honest and caring person always strives for an equitable exchange.

Equity is defined in this case as both parties walking away from the exchange satisfied with what they received. If you care about others, take time to figure out what constitutes an equitable exchange in any situation. Often all that's required in return is a thank you.

Why is Rule 7 relevant to leadership?

Mastering the art of the equitable exchange is a key leadership skill. As Napoleon once said, "Men are moved by only one of two levers—fear and self-interest." Self-interest can take many forms. It depends on the "currency" of the individual you're dealing with. Currency means what the other person expects in return for a service or favor. Currency can be anything—a smile and a thank-you, money, recognition, or extra time off from work.

When you strive to understand the currency of others, you become more focused on the equitable exchange and you learn what motivates people. Take an interest in learning the currency of everyone you deal with for each exchange. Most times it's simple and obvious. Other times, it takes some effort to understand what others want.

Here's some further context for Rule 7. It's intended to be applied in your interpersonal relationships as a leader. It's not intended to be used as a rule for business-to-business negotiations. Business negotiations have different rules that apply. Each party is responsible for establishing and pursing their own negotiating goals. However, even in a business negotiation, the best outcomes are those that seek a win-win result.

CHAPTER 8

Rule 8: Competition Is Healthy, Embrace It—The Right Way

"I have been up against tough competition all my life. I would-n't know how to get along without it."

— *Walt Disney*

If you received lots of trophies just for participating in sports or some other activity when you were a kid, I am profoundly grieved on your behalf. The parents probably got together and decided they didn't want any of the little kiddies to feel sad if they lost. So everyone got a trophy. I'm embarrassed to say that I also succumbed to this pressure occasionally when I was a youth sports coach, until a light bulb went on. If winning or losing was that irrelevant, why didn't we just shut off the scoreboard too?

The truth is that coming up empty-handed, even after you have given your best, is one of the most powerful lessons you can ever learn. You have to accept that such failures are nothing more than fuel for your future success. The world owes you nothing. The bit-ter taste of defeat is a powerful driver to improve and compete, with even more determination next time around.

Competition requires you to always improve and be better than you were yesterday. Everything around you is competitive to some degree. The entire ecosystem is a competition among species and so is everything in the economy. It's in your best interest to welcome and thrive on competition. The key is to always play by the rules of the game.

Compete with honor.

When I was a youth basketball coach, the league would recruit parent volunteers to assist with running the game clock and keeping the scorebook. One year, my team made it all the way to the championship game. The person keeping the scorebook for this game was the father of a young man on the opposing team. About three minutes into the game, I caught the scorekeeper volunteer cheating. He was shaving fouls, meaning that when his son's team would commit a foul, he simply wouldn't write it down—a nice advantage. After catching him red-handed, he denied it and claimed it was all a mistake, but I knew better. With his scheme exposed, my team eventually won the game and the championship.

I couldn't help but wonder, "What was he thinking? What in the world would he have gained if his son's team had won with the help of his cheating? Where is the honor in that kind of win, and what value does it have?"

If people would do this sort of thing in a youth basketball game, it's no wonder we have so many problems in the business world and society in general. I guess some people think it's just competition and you have to win by any means necessary. I wonder how that guy would feel if he were on the receiving end of his cheating scheme.

Compete fairly. Remember Rule 2? Keep it at the forefront of all your actions as you compete. Regardless of the outcome, always make sure you win or lose with your honor intact. Your wins will be much sweeter, and the bitterness of defeat will be lessened when you know you tried your best while playing by the rules.

Why is Rule 8 relevant to leadership?

Leaders must be strong competitors. They have to be driven because they in turn are the drivers of the team they lead. At the same time, leaders must compete with honor. In business, ethics and integrity violations of any sort are always soon discovered. When they are, the ensuing damage is often devastating to an organization, and the personal price you'll pay will make you wish you were never born.

Keep your commitment to the virtues of honor and honesty strong by minding the little things. If you can't be trusted with something small, you can't be trusted with something big. A strong sense of integrity starts with doing the right thing all the time.

What happened in the basketball game mentioned above served as the inspiration for my company tagline, "Lead Well and Win." It is indeed possible to lead with honor, compete fiercely, and still come out on top. I grew up with a strong sense of honor thanks to my father. That basketball game imprinted the principle in my heart forever.

CHAPTER 9

Rule 9: Self-Reliance is a Great Gift You Can Give Yourself

"Trust thyself: every heart vibrates to that iron string."

— *Ralph Waldo Emerson*

If you love yourself, be self-reliant. If you want to destroy your sense of self-worth, be perpetually dependent. Self-reliance is the highest form of self-esteem. When you believe in yourself and know you can stand on your own, you have the confidence to solve the problems life throws at you every day—most of them small, but some of them huge.

Self-reliance creates a sense of freedom that feeds the spirit. When you accomplish something, it's like completing a workout at the gym. You feel stronger. In fact, self-reliance is one of those skills I addressed in Rule 7 that generates value. Self-reliance fuels optimism for the attainment of any goal you set your mind to.

Businesses need problem solvers. Problem solvers are self-reliant people who take ownership of challenges. They don't phone home every time an obstacle crashes in their path. They carry conviction in their hearts that every problem has a solution and that the way forward will present itself.

Does self-reliance mean that you should never ask for help? Quite the contrary. The fastest way to learn is by studying the experience of others and asking for advice from a mentor. Why repeat past mistakes? We all need others on occasion, there's a big difference between occasionally needing a hand and being perpetually dependent.

How can you become self-reliant? For one thing, refuse handouts as the easy way out and make sure you earn your way through life by offering something of value in return for whatever you receive. If someone does give you a hand-out during a tough time, make sure to pay it back or pay it forward.

To become self-reliant, you have to stretch. By stretching I mean, put yourself in challenging situations where you will have to learn new skills and do things that you may not have done before. When you stretch outside your comfort zone, it generates tremendous personal growth.

Often I've accepted promotions and new assignments where my skills would be tested and success was by no means guaranteed. The new challenges provided all the teaching I needed. I had to solve problems and look for solutions wherever I could find them.

When you stretch, you will feel a certain amount of anxiety and fear. Overcoming this fear and pressing forward anyway is part of becoming self-reliant. As you grow and learn, you'll be less and less intimidated by new situations. You'll develop an inner core of confidence in overcoming obstacles. Before too long, fear and anxiety melt away and are no longer a factor when you reach for new goals.

Why is Rule 9 relevant to leadership?

Leaders promote a sense of self-reliance in the teams they lead. It's true that it takes a team to reach big, complex goals, but along the way, every major goal is divided into individual tasks that must be performed by each team member. Every team member must then have a mindset that they can indeed accomplish what's expected of them. Therefore, self-reliance is not isolationism. Self-reliance is a "can-do, will-do" attitude. It's a sense of confidence in yourself and your ability. You only develop this through exercise. The more you do, the stronger you become.

Whether in business or your personal life, dependence on external systems, organizations, and others as the solution to your problems is akin to living in a swamp. You'll sink slowly and something always stinks. The stink is your self-esteem rotting away. Don't let that happen. Become self-reliant.

CHAPTER 10

Rule 10: Stay Humble

"Humility is not thinking less of yourself, it's thinking of yourself less."

— *C. S. Lewis*

Always remember that no matter what your station is in life or how high you climb in the eyes of others, you will one day face the moment of your own demise. You won't be able to delegate this task. You'll do it by yourself, but hopefully you won't be alone when your moment comes. Money won't save you. Status will mean nothing. You'll simply slip away into the great beyond with nothing, just like the day you arrived. This thought always humbles me. It reminds me that there has to be more to life than being self-centered.

When you're young and have so much life and potential ahead of you, it's easy to ignore this perspective. The older you get, the more the things that really matter come into focus. The sooner you can accept this perspective, the more you'll be able to focus on what matters while discounting the things that have little value in the long run. Relationships with good people tend to become the most valuable part of life as you age. Humility helps to create those treasured relationships.

Why is Rule 10 relevant to leadership?

Being a leader requires a healthy ego. You obviously have to think highly of yourself to accept the responsibilities of leadership. You have to be as confident as a tightrope walker that you can succeed. But it's easy to let your ego swell to the point that it becomes a liability. The unchecked ego leads to selfishness and a sense that you are the center of the universe. This is total arrogance, which has been the downfall of many a great leader.

Humility keeps your ego in check. Reminding yourself that you are not the center of the universe is a great way to keep your ego healthy. When you let your ego swell, you start to think that you have no need for further learning. You start thinking too highly of yourself, and that leads to stagnation and an eventual flaming crash. When you're humble, you always view yourself as a work in progress that has room for improvement. Humility keeps you sharp in all aspects of life.

As a leader, are you willing to take a daily teaspoon of humility as the antidote to arrogance? I hope so, because otherwise life will deliver humility through a fire hose when you least expect it. Humility keeps the ego focused on developing authentic leadership presence.

Nothing is more effective as a reminder to remain humble than our temporary status on earth. This makes Rule 2 seem that much more important, doesn't it? Gee, as I think about it, everything seems to lead back to that pesky Rule 2.

Rule 2—Focus on the Big Stuff

"'Love the Lord your God with all your heart and with all your soul and with all your mind.' This is the first and greatest commandment. And the second is like it: 'Love your neighbor as yourself.' All the Law and the Prophets hang on these two commandments."

— Jesus Christ

You Are the Sculptor of Your Life

"Every block of stone has a statue inside it, and it is the task of the sculptor to discover it."

— *Michelangelo Buonarroti*

Nearly everyone hates rules. Yet, we are always governed by the rules of the natural world, whether we are aware of them or not. We live under rules such as the Law of Gravity, Laws of Motion, and Laws of Thermodynamics. We are constrained by the laws that are irrevocably etched into nature. When we attempt to defy these laws, we quickly run into trouble.

Yet when we learn to work with these laws, we achieve remarkable things, though it takes tremendous amounts of energy to do so. Think of a rocket launching into space. It uses all three laws to its advantage, yet if the engines should "flame out" or fail, the natural laws overwhelm it with catastrophic results.

Comparably, the *Ten Timeless Rules for Life* are your "laws" for living harmoniously and thriving in the world. They span the generations and all forms of human society. Just like the rocket that soars into space, you can apply the *Ten Timeless Rules for Life* to make your own perfect launch. It will take your energy to make it all happen and avoid engine failure.

Let's mix in another metaphor just for fun. You are the sculptor of your life. The extraordinary artist Michelangelo would look at a block of stone and imagine the figure "trapped" within it. Michelangelo simply saw it as his job to free the figure trapped inside the marble. Another artist might see an entirely different figure and that's okay. Still, another much less imaginative artist might see no figure at all. Such was the case with the block of marble that ultimately became the famous sculpture of David.

The colossal block of marble he used was discarded by other artists as inferior because of the many imperfections that were visible in the stone. It sat unused for 25 years before Michelangelo saw it. He had a different, far more dynamic vision and saw ways he could work around the imperfections and put the marble to good use. Because of his fervent imagination, he was able to create what is regarded by many as the greatest artistic masterpiece of all time.

We are all blocks of marble with imperfections, but each of us contains a masterpiece inside us. It's a tragedy when we can't see past the imperfections and we throw away our own lives or dismiss others as useless. The masterpiece remains trapped forever.

As Michelangelo chipped away at the marble for the four years it took to finish his project, he applied tools and techniques that were the foundation for his mastery. The *Ten Timeless Rules for Life* are your tools and techniques. Let them be the foundation for your life. Commit to creating your masterpiece, that one of a kind creation that no one else can copy—the best you that can possibly be.

Index

ABOUT THE AUTHOR

When I was in college, I discovered leadership. I went to see an Army recruiter about joining ROTC. As he was outlining the benefits of an Army career, he said the words that changed my life, "We'll make you a leader." I've been fascinated by leadership ever since. I served four years in the Army before transitioning to private industry.

I ultimately became a vice president at a major technology company until I decided to start my own company, 4 Power Leadership, so I could teach leadership principles to others. Dedicating myself to being a good leader has helped my career flourish and motivated me to uphold high personal standards.

If you would like to invite me to speak to your group, I'd welcome the opportunity. Simply send an email to inquiry@4powerleadership.com. Whether it's an invitation to speak or you have comments on this book, I'd love to hear from you, and I'll do my best to answer any questions you might have.

www.ingramcontent.com/pod-product-compliance
Lightning Source LLC
Chambersburg PA
CBHW060202070426
42447CB00033B/2289